CALIFORNIA
NATIVE AMERICAN TRIBES

TOLOWA TRIBE

by Mary Null Boulé

Book Twenty in a series of twenty-six

Dear Reader,

You will find an outline of this chapter's important topics at the back of the booklet. It is there for you to use in writing a report or giving an oral report on this tribe.

If you first read the booklet completely, then you can use the outline as a guide to write your report in your own words, instead of copying sentences from the chapter.

Good luck, read carefully, and use your own words.

MNB

Cover Illustration: Daniel Liddell

CALIFORNIA NATIVE AMERICAN TRIBES

TOLOWA TRIBE

by
Mary Null Boulé

Illustrated by
Daniel Liddell

Merryant Publishing
Vashon, Washington

Book Number Twenty in a series of twenty-six

This series is dedicated to Virginia Harding, whose editing expertise and friendship brought this project to fruition.

ISBN: 1-877599-43-3

Copyright © 1992, Merryant Publishing

7615 S.W. 257th St., Vashon, WA 98070.

FOREWORD

Native American people of the United States are often living their lives away from major cities and away from what we call the mainstream of life. It is, then, interesting to learn of the important part these remote tribal members play in our everyday lives.

More than 60% of our foods come from the ancient Native American's diet. Farming methods of today also can be traced back to how tribal women grew crops of corn and grain. Many of our present day ideas of democracy have been taken from tribal governments. Even some 1,500 Native American words are found in our English language today.

Fur traders bought furs from tribal hunters for small amounts of money, sold them to Europeans and Asians for a great deal of money, and became rich. Using their money to buy land and to build office buildings, some traders started business corporations which are now the base of our country's economy.

There has never been enough credit given to these early Americans who took such good care of our country when it was still in their care. The time has come to realize tribal contributions to our society today and to give Native Americans not only the credit, but the respect due them.

Mary Boulé

A-frame cradle for girls; tule matting. Tubatulabal tribe.

GENERAL INFORMATION

Out of Asia, many thousands of years ago, came Wanderers. Some historians think they were the first people to set foot on our western hemisphere. These Wanderers had walked, step by step, onto our part of the earth while hunting and gathering food. They probably never even knew they had moved from one continent to another as they made their way across a land bridge, a narrow strip of land between Siberia and what is now Russia, and the state of Alaska.

Historians do not know exactly how long ago the Wanderers might have crossed the land bridge. Some of them say 35,000 years ago. What historians do know is that these people slowly moved down onto land that we now call the United States of America. Today it would be very hard to follow their footsteps, for the land bridge has been covered with sea water since the thawing of the ice age.

Those Wanderers who made their way to California were very lucky, indeed. California was a land with good weather most of the year and was filled with plenty of plant and animal foods for them to eat.

The Wanderers who became California's Native Americans did not organize into large tribes like the rest of the North American tribes. Instead, they divided into groups, or tribelets, sometimes having as many as 250 people. A tribelet could number as few as three, to as many as thirty villages located close to each other. Some tribelets had only one chief, a leader who lived in the largest village. Many tribes had a chief for each village. Some leaders had no real power but were thought to be wise. Tribal members always listened with respect to what their chief had to say.

From 20 to 100 people could be living in one village, which usually had several houses. In most cases, these groups of people were related to each other. From five to ten people of one family lived in one house. For instance, a mother, a father, two or three children, a grandmother, or aunt or daughter-in-law might live together.

Village members together would own the land important to them for their well-being. Their land might include oak trees with precious acorns, streams and rivers, and plants which were good to eat. Streams and rivers were especially important to a tribe's quality of life. Water drew animals to it; that meant more food for the tribe to eat. Fish were a good source of food, and traveling by boat was often easier than walking long distances. Water was needed in every part of tribal life.

Village and tribelet land was carefully guarded. Each group knew exactly where the boundaries of its land were found. Boundaries were known by landmarks such as mountains or rivers, or they might also be marked by poles planted in the ground. Some boundary lines were marked by rocks, or by objects placed there by tribal members. The size of a territory had to be large enough to supply food to every person living there.

The California tribes spoke many languages. Sometimes villages close together even had a problem understanding one another. This meant that each group had to be sure of the boundaries of other tribes around them when gathering food. It would not be wise to go against the boundaries and the customs of neighbors. The Native Americans found if they respected the boundaries of their neighbors, not so many wars had to be fought. California tribes, in spite of all their differences, were not as warlike as other tribes in our country.

Not only did the California tribes speak different languages, but their members also differed in size. Some tribes were very tall, almost six feet tall. The shortest people came from the Yuki tribe which had territory in what is now Mendocino County. They measured only about 5'2" tall. All Native Americans, regardless of size, had strong, straight black hair and dark brown eyes.

TRADE

Trading between tribes was an important part of life. Inland tribes had large animal hides that coastal tribes wanted. By trading the hides to coastal groups, inland tribes would receive fish and shells, which they in turn wanted. Coastal tribes also wanted minerals and rocks mined in the mountains by inland tribes. Obsidian rock from the northern mountains was especially wanted for arrowheads. There were, as well, several minerals, mined in the inland mountains, which could be made into the colorful body paints needed for religious ceremonies.

Southern tribes particularly wanted steatite from the Gabrielino tribe. Steatite, or soapstone, was a special metal which allowed heat to spread evenly through it. This made it a good choice to be used for cooking pots and flat frying pans. It could be carved into bowls because of its softness and could be decorated by carving designs into it. Steatite came from Catalina Island in the Coastal Gabrielino territory. Gabrielinos found steatite to be a fine trading item to offer for the acorns, deerskins, or obsidian stone they needed.

When people had no items to trade but needed something, they used small strings of shells for money. The small dentalium shells, which came from the far distant Northwest coast, had great value. Strings of dentalia usually served as money in the Northern California tribes, although some dentalia was used in the Central California tribes.

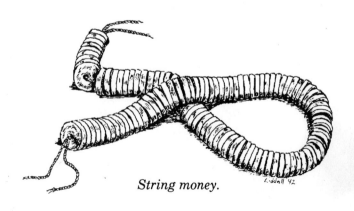

String money.

In southern California clam shells were broken and holes were bored through the center of each piece. Then the pieces were rounded and polished with sandstone and strung into strings for money. These were not thought to be as valuable as dentalia.

Strings of shell money were measured by tattoo marks on the trader's lower arm or hand.

Here is a sample of shell value:

A house, three strings
A fishing place, one to three strings
Land with acorn-bearing oak trees, one to five strings

A great deal of rock and stone was traded among the tribes for making tools. Arrows had to have sharp-edged stone for tips. The best stone for arrow tips was obsidian (volcanic glass) because, when hit properly, it broke off into flakes with very sharp edges. California tribes considered obsidian to be the most valuable rock for trading.

Some tribes had craftsmen who made knives with wooden handles and obsidian blades. Often the handles were decorated with carvings. Such knives were good for trading purposes. Stone mortars and pestles, used by the women for grinding grains into flour, were good trading items.

BASKETS & POTTERY

California tribal women made beautiful baskets. The Pomo and Chumash baskets, what few are left, show us that the women of those tribes might have been some of the finest basketmakers in the world. Baskets were used for gathering and storing food, for carrying babies, and even for hauling water. In emergencies, such as flooding waters, sometimes children, women, and tribal belongings crossed the swollen rivers and streams in huge, woven baskets! Baskets were so tightly woven that not a drop of water could leak from them.

Baskets also made fine cooking pots. Very hot rocks were taken from a fire and tossed around inside baskets with a looped tree branch until food in the basket was cooked.

Most baskets were made to do a certain job, but some baskets were designed for their beauty alone and were excellent for trading. Older women of a tribe would teach young girls how to weave baskets.

Pottery was not used by many California tribes. What little there was seems to have been made by those tribes living near to the Navaho and Mohave tribes of Arizona, and it shows their style. For example, pottery of the California tribes did not have much decoration and was usually a dull red color. Designs were few and always in yellow.

Ohlone hunter wearing deerskin camouflage.

Long thin coils of clay were laid one on top the other. Then the coils were smoothed between a wooden paddle and a small stone to shape the bowl. Pottery from California Native Americans has been described as light weight and brittle (easily broken), probably because of the kind of clay soil found in California.

HUNTING & FISHING

Tribal men spent much of their time making hunting and fishing tools. Bows and arrows were built with great care, to make them shoot as accurately as possible. Carelessly made hunting weapons caused fewer animals to be killed and people then had less food to eat.

Bows made by men of Southern California tribes were made long and narrow. In the northern part of the state bows were a little shorter, thinner, and wider than those of their northern neighbors. Size and thickness of bows depended on the size trees growing in a tribe's territory. The strongest bows were wrapped with sinew, the name given to animal tendons. Sinew is strong and elastic like a rubber band.

Arrows were made in many sizes and shapes, depending on their use. For hunting larger animals, a two-piece arrow was used. The front piece of the arrow shaft was made so that it would remain in the animal, even if the back part was

9

removed or broken off. The arrowhead, or point, was wrapped to the front piece of the shaft. This kind of arrow was also used in wars.

Young boys used a simple wooden arrow with the end sharpened to a point. With this they could hunt small animals like birds and rabbits. The older men of the tribe taught boys how to make their own arrows, how to aim properly, and how to repair broken weapons.

Tribal men spent many hours making and mending fishing nets. The string used in making nets often came from the fibers of plants. These fibers were twisted to make them strong and tough, then knotted into netting. Fences, or weirs, that had one small opening for fish, were built across streams. As the fish swam through the opening they would be caught in netting or harpooned by a waiting fisherman.

Hooks, if used at all, were cut from shells. Mostly hooks could be found when the men fished in large lakes or when catching trout in high mountain areas. Hooks were attached to heavy plant fiber string.

Dip nets, made of netting attached to branches that were bent into a circle, were used to catch fish swimming near shore. Dip nets had long handles so the fishermen could reach deep into the water.

Sometimes a mild poison was placed on the surface of shallow water. This confused the fish and caused them to float to the surface of the water, where they could be scooped up by a waiting fisherman. Not enough poison was used to make humans ill.

Not all fishing was done from the shore. California tribes used two kinds of boats when fishing. Canoes, dug out of one half a log, were useful for river fishing. These were square at each end, round on the bottom, and very heavy. Some of them were well-finished, often even having a carved seat in them.

Today we think of "balsa" as a very lightweight wood, but in Spanish, the word balsa means "raft". That is why Spanish explorers called the Native American canoes, made from tule reeds, "balsa" boats.

Balsa boats were made of bundled tule reeds and were used throughout most of California. They made into safe, lightweight boats for lake and river use. Usually the balsa canoe had a long, tightly tied bundle of tule for the boat bottom and one bundle for each side of the canoe. The front of the canoe was higher than the back. Balsa boats could be steered with a pole or with a paddle, like a raft.

Men did most of the fishing, women were in charge of gathering grasses, seeds, and acorns for food. After the food was collected, it was either eaten right away or made ready for winter storage.

Except for a few southern groups, California tribes had permanent villages where they lived most of the year. They also had food-gathering places they returned to each year to collect acorns, salt, fish, and other foods not found near their villages.

FOOD

Many different kinds of plant food grew wild in California in the days before white people arrived. Berries and other plant foods grew in the mountains. Forests offered the local tribes everything from pine nuts to animals.

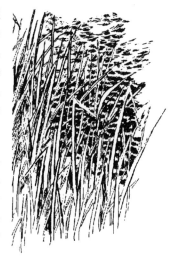

Native Americans found streams full of fish for much of the year. Inland fresh water lakes had large tule reeds growing along their shores. Tule could be eaten as food when plants were young and tender. More important, however, tule was used in making fabric for clothes and for building boats and houses. Tule was probably the most useful plant the California Native Americans found growing wild in their land.

Like all deserts, the one in southern California had little water or fish, but small animals and cactus plants made good food for the local tribes. They moved from place to place harvesting whatever was ripe. Tribal members always knew when and where to find the best food in their territory.

Acorns were the main source of food for all California tribes. Acorn flour was as important to the California Native Americans as wheat is to us today. Five types of California oak trees produced acorns that could be eaten. Those from black oak and tanbark oak seem to have been the favorite kinds.

Since some acorns tasted better than others, the tastiest ones were collected first. If harvest of the favorite acorn was poor some years, then less tasty acorns had to be eaten all winter long.

So important were acorns to California Indians that most tribes built their entire year around them. Acorn harvest marked the beginning of their calendar year. Winter was counted as so many months after acorn harvest, and summer was counted by the number of months before the next acorn harvest.

Acorn harvest ceremonies usually were the biggest events of the year. Most celebrations took place in mid-October and included dancing, feasts, games of chance, and reunions with relatives. Harvest festivals lasted for many days. They were a time of joy for everyone.

The annual acorn gathering lasted two to three weeks. Young boys climbed the oak trees to shake branches; some men used long poles to knock acorns to the ground. Women loaded the nuts into large cone-shaped burden baskets and carried them to a central place where they were put in the sun to dry.

Once the acorns were dried, the women carried them back to the tribe's permanent villages. There they lined special basket-like storage granaries with strong herbs to keep insects away, then stored the acorns inside. Granaries were placed on stilts to keep animals from getting into them and were kept beside tribal houses.

Preparing acorns for each meal was also the women's job. Shells were peeled by hitting the acorns with a stone hammer on an anvil (flat) stone. Meat from the nut was then laid on a stone mortar. A mortar was usually a large stone with a slight dip on its surface. Sometimes the mortar had a bottomless basket, called a hopper, glued to its top. This kept the acorn meat from sliding off the mortar as it was beaten. The meat was then pounded with a long stone pestle. Acorn flour was scraped away from the hopper's sides with a soaproot fiber brush during this process.

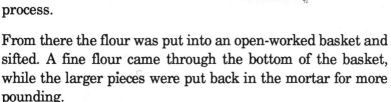

From there the flour was put into an open-worked basket and sifted. A fine flour came through the bottom of the basket, while the larger pieces were put back in the mortar for more pounding.

The most important process came after the acorn flour was sifted. Acorn flour has a very bitter-tasting tannin in it. This bitter taste was removed by a method called leaching. Many tribes leached the flour by first scooping out a hollow in sand near water. The hollow was lined with leaves to keep the flour from washing away. A great deal of hot water was poured through the flour to wash out (leach) the bitterness. Sometimes the flour was put into a basket for the leaching process, instead of using sand and leaves.

Finally the acorn flour was ready to be cooked. To make mush, heated stones were placed in the basket with the flour. A looped tree branch or two long sticks were used to toss the hot rocks around so the basket would not burn. When the mush had boiled, it could be eaten. If the flour and water mixture was baked in an earthen oven, it became a kind of bread. Early explorers wrote that it was very tasty.

Historians have estimated that one family would eat from 1500 to 2000 pounds of acorn flour a year. One reason California native Americans did not have to plant seeds and raise crops was because there were so many acorns for them to harvest each year.

Whether they ate fish or shellfish or plant food or animal meat, nature supplied more than enough food for the Native Americans who lived in California long ago. Many believed their good fortune in having fine weather and plenty to eat came from being good to their gods.

RELIGION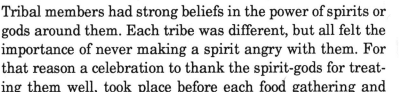

Tribal members had strong beliefs in the power of spirits or gods around them. Each tribe was different, but all felt the importance of never making a spirit angry with them. For that reason a celebration to thank the spirit-gods for treating them well, took place before each food gathering and before each hunting trip, and after each food harvest.

Usually spiritual powers were thought to belong to birds or animals. Most California tribespeople felt bears were very wicked and should not be eaten. But Coyote seems to have been a kind leader who helped them if they were in trouble, even though he seems to have been a bit naughty at times. Eagle was thought to be very powerful and good to native Americans. In some tribes, Eagle was almost as powerful as Sun.

Tribes placed importance on different gods, according to the tribe's needs. Rain gods were the most important spirits to desert tribes. Weather gods, who might bring less rain or warmer temperatures, were important to northern tribes. A great many groups felt there were gods for each of the winds: North, South, East and West. The four directions were usually included in their ceremonial dances and were used as part of the decorations on baskets, pots, and even tools.

Animals were not only worshipped and believed to be spirit-gods, like Deer or Antelope, but tribal members felt there was a personal animal guardian for each one of them. If a tribal member had a deer as guardian, then that person could never kill a deer or eat deer meat.

California Native Americans believed in life after death. This made them very respectful of death and very fearful of angering a dead person. Once someone died, the name of the dead person could never again be said aloud. Since it was easy to accidentally say a name aloud, the name was usually given to a new baby. Then the dead person would not become angry.

Shamans were thought to be the keepers of religious beliefs and to have the ability to talk directly to spirit-gods. It was the job of a village shaman to cure sick people, and to speak to the gods about the needs of the people. Some tribes had several kinds of shamans in one village. One shaman did curing, one scared off evil spirits, while another took care of hunters.

Not all shamans were nice, so people greatly feared their power. However, if shamans had no luck curing sick people or did not bring good luck in hunting, the people could kill them. Most shamans were men, but in a few tribes, women were doctors.

Most California tribal myths have been lost to history because they were spoken and never written down. The legends were told and retold on winter nights around the home fires. Sadly, these were forgotten after the missionaries brought Christianity to California and moved tribal members into the missions.

A few stories still remain, however. It is thought by historians that northwest California tribes were the only ones not to have a myth on how they were created. They did not feel that the world was made and prepared for human beings. Instead, their few remaining stories usually tell of mountain peaks or rivers in their own territory.

The central California tribes had creation stories of a great flood where there was only water on earth. They tell of how man was made from a bit of mud that a turtle brought up from the bottom of the water.

Many southwest tribes believed there was a time of no sky or water. They told of two clouds appearing which finally became Sky and Earth.

Throughout California, however, all tribes had myths that told of Eagle as the leader, Coyote as chief assistant, and of less powerful spirits like Falcon or Hawk.

Costumes for religious ceremonies often imitated these animals they worshipped or feared. Much time was spent in making the dance costumes as beautiful as possible. Red woodpecker feathers were so brilliant a color they were used to decorate religious headdresses, necklaces, or belts. Deerskin clothing was fringed so shell beads could be attached to each thin strip of leather.

Eagle feathers were felt to be the most sacred of religious objects. Sometimes they were made into whole robes.

Religious feather charm.

Usually, though, the feathers were used just for decorations. All these costumes were valuable to the people of each tribe. The village chief was in charge of taking care of the costumes, and there was terrible punishment for stealing them. Clothing worn everyday was not fancy like costuming for rituals.

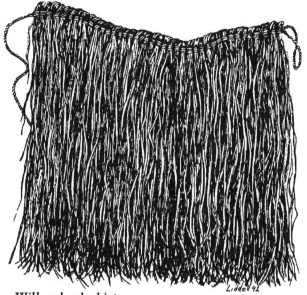

Willow bark skirt.

CLOTHING

Central and southern California's fine weather made regular clothes not really very important to the Native Americans. The children and men went naked most of the year, but most women wore a short apron-like skirt. These skirts were usually made in two pieces, front and back aprons, with fringes cut into the bottom edges. Often the skirt was made from the inner bark of trees, shredded and gathered on a cord. Sometimes the skirt was made from tule or grass.

In northern California and in rainy or windy weather elsewhere in the state, animal-skin blankets were worn by both men and women. They were used like a cape and wrapped around the body. Sometimes the cape was put over one shoulder and under the other arm, then tied in front. All kinds of skins were used; deer, otter, wildcat, but sea-otter fur was thought to be the best. If the skin was from a small animal, it was cut into strips and woven together into a fabric. At night the cape became a blanket to keep the person warm.

Because of the rainy weather in northern California, the women wore basket caps all the time. Women of the central and south tribes wore caps only when carrying heavy loads, where the forehead had to be used as support. Then a cap helped keep too much weight from being placed on the forehead.

Most California people went barefoot in their villages. For journeys into rough land, going to war, wood gathering, or in colder weather, the tribesmen in central and northwest California wore a one-piece soft shoe with no extra sole, which went high up on the leg.

Southern California tribespeople, however, wore sandals most of the time, wearing high, soled moccasins only when they traveled long distances or into the mountains. Leggings of skin were worn in snow, and moccasins were sometimes lined with grass for more comfort and warmth.

VILLAGE LIFE

Houses of the California tribes were made of materials found in their area. Usually they were round with domed roofs. Except for a few tribes, a house floor was dug into the earth a few feet. This was wise, for it made the home warmer in winter and cooler in summer. It also meant that less material was needed to make house walls.

Framework for the walls was made from bendable branches tied to support poles. Some frames of the houses were covered with earth and grass. Others were covered with large slabs of redwood or pine bark. Central California

Split-stick clapper, rhythm instrument. Hupa tribe.

villagers made large woven mats of tule reed to cover the tops and sides of houses. In the warmer southern area, brush and smaller pieces of bark were used for house walls.

Most California Native American villages had a building called a sweathouse, where the men could be found when they were not hunting, fishing or traveling. It was a very important place for the men, who used it rather like a clubhouse. They could sweat and then scrape themselves clean with curved ribs of deer. The sweathouse was smaller than a family house. Normally it had a center pole framework with a firepit on the ground next to the pole. When the fire was lit, some smoke was allowed to escape through a hole at the top of the roof; however, most was trapped inside the building. Smoke and heat were the main reasons for having a sweathouse. Both were believed to be a way to purify tribal members' bodies. Sweathouse walls were mainly hard-packed earth. The heat produced was not a steam heat but came from a wood-fed fire.

In the center of most villages was a large house that often had no walls, just a roof held up with poles. It was here that religious dances and rituals were held, or visitors were entertained.

Dances were enjoyed and were performed with great skill. Music, usually only rhythm instruments, accompanied the dances. For some reason California Native Americans did not use drums to create rhythms for their dances. Three different kinds of rattles were used by California tribes.

One type, split-clap sticks, created rhythm for dancing. These were usually a length of cane (a hollow stick) split in half lengthwise for about two-thirds of its length. The part still uncut was tightly wound with cord so it would not split all the way. The stick was held at the tied end in one hand and hit against the palm of the other hand to make its sound.

19

A pebble-filled moth cocoon made rhythm for shaman duties. These could range from calling on spirits to cure illnesses, to performing dances to bring rain. Probably the best sounds to beat rhythm for songs and dances came from bundles of deer hooves tied together on a stick. These rattles have a hollow, warm sound.

The only really "musical" instrument found in California was a flute made of reed that was played by blowing across the edge of one end. Melodies were not played on any of these instruments. Most North American Indians sang their songs rather than playing melodies on music instruments.

Special songs were sung for each event. There were songs for healing sick people, songs for success in hunting, war, or marriage. Women sang acorn-grinding songs and lullabies. Songs were sung in sorrow for the dead and during story-telling times. Group singing, with a leader, was the favorite kind of singing. Most songs were sung by all tribe members, but religious songs had to be sung by a special group. It was important that sacred songs not be changed through the years. If a mistake was made while singing sacred music, the singer could be punished, so only specially trained singers would sing ritual songs.

All songs were very short, some of them only 20 to 30 seconds long. They were made longer by repeating the melodies over and over, or by connecting several songs together. Songs usually told no story, just repeated words or phrases or syllables in patterns.

Song melodies used only one or two notes and harmony was never added. Perhaps that is why mission Indians, at those missions with musician priests, especially loved to sing harmony in the church choirs.

Songs and dances were good methods of passing rich tribal traditions on to the children. It was important to tribal adults that their children understand and love the tribe's heritage.

Children were truly wanted by parents in most tribes and new parents carefully watched their tiny babies day and night, to be sure they stayed warm and dry. Usually a newborn was strapped into a cradle and tied to the mother's back so she could continue to work, yet be near the baby at all times. In some tribes, older children took care of babies of cradle age during the day to give the mother time to do all her work, while grandmothers were often in charge of caring for toddlers.

Children were taught good behavior, traditions, and tribal rules from babyhood, although some tribes were stricter than others. Most of the time parents made their children obey. Young children could be lightly punished, but in many tribes those over six or seven years old were more severely punished if they did not follow the rules.

Just as children do today, Native American youngsters had childhood traditions they followed. For instance, one tribal tradition said that when a baby tooth came out, a child waited until dusk, faced the setting sun and threw the tooth to the west. There is no mention of a generous tooth fairy, however.

Tribal parents were worried that their offspring might not be strong and brave. Some tribes felt one way to make their children stronger was by forcing them to bathe in ice cold water, even in wintertime. Every once in a while, for example, Modoc children were awakened from sleep and taken to a cold lake or stream for a freezing bath.

But if freezing baths at night were hard on young Native Americans, their days were carefree and happy. Children were allowed to play all day, and some tribes felt children did not even have to come to dinner if they didn't want to. In those tribes, children could come to their houses to eat anytime of the day.

The games boys played are not too different from those played today. Swimming, hide and seek among the tule reeds, a form of tetherball with a mud ball tied to a pole, and willow-javelin throwing kept boys busy throughout the day.

Fathers made their sons small bows and arrows, so boys spent much time trying to improve their hunting skills. They practised shooting at frogs or chipmunks. The first animal any boy killed was not touched or eaten by him. Others would carry the kill home to be cooked and eaten by villagers. This tradition taught boys always to share food.

Another hunting tool for boys was a hollowed-out willow branch. This became like a modern day beanshooter, only the Native American boys shot juniper berries instead of beans. Slingshots made good hunting weapons, as well.

Girls and boys shared many games, but girls playing with each other had contests to see who could make a basket the fastest, or they played with dolls made of tule. Together, young boys and girls played a type of ring-around-the-rosie game, climbed mountains, or built mud houses.

As children grew older, the boys followed their fathers and the girls followed their mothers as the adults did their daily work. Children were not trained in the arts of hunting or basketmaking, however, until they became teenagers.

HISTORY

Spanish missionaries, led by Fray Junipero Serra, arrived in California in 1769 to build missions along the coast of California. By 1823, fifty years later, 21 missions had been founded. Almost all of them were very successful, and the Franciscan monks who ran them were proud of how many Native Americans became Christians.

However, all was not as the monks had planned it would be. Native American people had never been around the diseases European white men brought with them. As a result, they had no immunity to such illnesses as measles, small pox, or flu. Too many mission Indians died from white men's diseases.

Historians figure there were 300,000 Native Americans living in California before the missionaries came. The missions show records of 83,000 mission Indians during mission days. By the time the Mexicans took over the missions from the Spanish in 1834, only 20,000 remained alive.

The great California Gold Rush of 1849 was probably another big reason why many of the Native Americans died during that time. White men, staking their claim to tribal lands with gold upon it, thought nothing of killing any California tribesman who tried to keep and protect his territory. Fifty-thousand tribal members died from diseases, bullets, or starvation between the gold Rush Days and 1870. By 1910, only 17,000 California Indians remained.

Although the American government tried to set aside reservations (areas reserved for Native Americans), the land given to the Indians often was not good land. Worse yet, some of the land sacred to tribes, such as burial grounds, was taken over by white people and never given back.

Sadly, mission Indians, when they became Christians, forgot the proud heritage and beliefs they had followed for thousands of years. Many wonderful myths and songs they had passed from one generation to the next, on winter nights so long ago, have been lost forever.

Today some 100,000 people can claim California Native American ancestors, but few pure-blooded tribespeople remain. Our link with the Wanderers, who came from Asia so long ago, has been forever broken.

The bullroarer made a deep, loud sound when whirled above the player's head. Tipai tribe.

Villages were usually built beside a lake, stream, or river. Balsa canoes are on the shore. Tule reeds grow along the edge of the water and are drying on poles on the right side of the picture.

Women preparing food in baskets, sit on tule mats. Tule mats are being tied to the willow pole framework of a house being built by one of the men.

TOLOWA TRIBE

INTRODUCTION

The Tolowa (Toe' luh wuh) tribal territory was in the far northwest corner of what is now the state of California. The Tolowa tribal name was given to them by the neighboring Yuroks. Some historians think it must have come from the name of one large Tolowan village. Other researchers feel the name came from a Yurok word *ni-tolowa,* which means "I speak Athabascan (a language spoken by Tolowa tribal members) of the Tolowa variety."

The tribe's northern boundary began at the mouth of the Winchuck River, just barely into Oregon, and went south to 17 miles beyond the present-day town of Crescent City, California. Their land spread inland, to the east, about twenty miles.

This small territory of only 640 square miles had four entirely different regions of land. Each region had its own plant life and climate. The coastal strip was sandy and treeless with rocky beaches. Tribal foods found in this area were mainly sea mammals and seaweed, which supplied the tribe not only with food but with salt for seasoning.

A second region lay next to the coast. It was a narrow band of redwood forests growing on low, hilly land, and a few larger animals were found living there. The third region was also forest land, but trees of this forest were Douglas fir and oak. The many oak trees furnished Tolowans with their basic food, acorns. This area was flat land surrounded by the high Siskiyou Mountains.

The fourth region of Tolowa territory was along the banks of the Smith River. This area was marshland, where the tall useful tule cane grew. Its streams, and the river itself, were full of salmon and eels.

Most of the permanent villages were found in the coastal strip of land. Each of the eight large villages there were known to have a population of between 100 and 300 people.

There was much visiting between villages. Every village had some coastal property, and whenever whales or sea lions washed ashore, tribal law said the meat from them belonged to the village that owned that bit of beach. This was an important way to keep relations with other villages peaceful.

Villagers stayed in their coastal houses through the rainy winters and for most of the rest of the year. They left their homes only for inland trips, beginning in August, to catch salmon in the river and to gather acorns in the high valleys. Tolowa people seldom went more than 15 miles from their village.

Even during food-gathering time, the coastal village was not left completely alone for several weeks at a time. Tribal women kept returning again and again with their heavy loads of dried fish and acorns to store them in village storage granaries.

Tall tule cane — used for clothing, houses, baskets — grows in marshland.

VILLAGES

Tolowa houses were made out of redwood planks and were sturdy, square homes, looking much like those built by northern tribes of Alaska and Washington. Roofs of these dwelling houses were steep and made of thick redwood planks. Outer house walls were made of upright planks and measured 15 feet long on each side.

Dwelling houses were built over a square foundation hole, dug two or three feet into the ground, that was only 10 feet on each side. This left a wide ledge of dirt inside the house, around the top edge of the foundation hole. Basket storage containers and belongings were stored on this shelf.

A few feet inside the doorway wall, another wall of the same size and height was built Firewood needed for the cold winter months was stored in this area. A fire pit for cooking and heating was placed in the center of the dwelling. Wives, unmarried daughters, and small children lived and slept in a dwelling house.

A sweathouse was found in each village. This was an almost completely underground area that had only one slanted roof wall showing above ground. It was used by village men not only as a place to sweat, but was also where village men and boys slept, made and repaired tools, and spent their free time.

A sweathouse was heated by a large wood fire, making the temperature inside hot enough to cause men to sweat. Sweating was believed to be the way to purify their bodies.

Each village had a special area where men made stone tools, split wood, or cleaned fish. A cemetery was found in every settlement, as well, usually placed a distance away from the village.

A Tolowa house.

VILLAGE LIFE

The Tolowa tribe had no chief over all its people, nor were there village councils. Each village was led by a headman, who was usually one of the wealthy villagers. Since wealth could be inherited from relatives in this tribe, the job of headman usually went to the son of a headman who had died.

Tolowa tribal members who owned obsidian (volcanic glass used for knife blades and arrow points), red woodpecker scalps, and dentalium shells were considered rich by other villagers. The more wealth a man had, the more powerful he was felt to be. Villagers worked hard to gain wealth and power.

Obsidian knife blade.

Rich tribal members were called on to settle problems between villagers, or between their village and other tribelets. All punishment for crimes, no matter how bad, was settled by criminals paying fines. Murder was settled by the murderer paying a big fine, while a crime of accidentally injuring someone was settled with a smaller payment. Fines were paid to those people who were wronged.

Even disobeying a tribal law was cause for paying a fine. For example, a villager who did not give the right to kill the first sea lion of the season to someone who had lost a close relative, was forced to pay 'money' (strings of shell beads) to the mourner. Saying aloud the name of a dead person was another taboo resulting in a fine having to be paid.

Needless to say, villagers watched each other closely to see if they could catch those who did something wrong. If criminals were too poor to pay their fines with money, the debts had to be paid by working for their victims. However, in the Tolowa tribe this kind of punishment was not so much slavery, it was more like a wronged person 'adopting' someone who owed them money.

The Tolowa people did not fight wars but sometimes got into serious arguments with fellow Tolowa villages or with the Yurok tribe. The only way to settle these kinds of problems was to have meetings, led by wealthy villagers, where both sides figured out a price of peace. Peace could be bought between villages and other tribes, just as it could between individuals.

Village headmen were in charge of ceremonies and dance events, paying for the cost of food and gifts to visitors themselves. They also loaned out fancy costumes to poor villagers for dances. Rich villagers saw to it that poorer families had food at all times. A wealthy man wore a small, decorated plug in his nose to let everyone know of his importance and power.

Decorated nose plug.

One of the ways a man could become wealthy was to have several daughters. Women were considered very important to the Tolowas because of the many jobs they did to feed and clothe their families. Therefore, young men, when they wanted a bride, had to pay a 'bride price' to the father of his chosen woman.

When a child was born to a couple, no rituals were celebrated. The child was usually not named until it was older. Wealthy people gave very fancy child-naming parties when their children were ready to be named, serving a feast to those invited to the party. Often poorer children were named at the these events, as well.

Many times the names given to children were those of villagers who had died. That way, if the name of a dead person was accidentally said aloud, a fine would not have to be paid.

There were no ceremonies for boys at teenage. Girls had their chins tattooed with three straight vertical lines at about the time they became teenagers.

Although there were no big celebrations for teenagers, there were many rituals and ceremonies when a villager died. Bodies were wrapped in woven tule mats and removed through a hole made in one wall of the house where they had died. Bodies were never carried through a doorway.

The body was unwrapped at a special area and washed, along with all its belongings (including valuable dentalia shells.) After rewrapping everything in tule mats, the body and its belongings were carried to the village cemetery and buried.

From the time of death until the burial, all village pleasure activities were stopped. Any visitor coming through the village at that time had to pay a fine.

RITUALS AND CEREMONIES

Most rituals performed by Tolowa tribal members had to do with food. The first catch of salmon, eels, and especially sea lions were all celebrated. The sea-lion event involved many coastal villages celebrating together. At the end of the ceremony, large canoes filled with tribal men were rowed into the ocean to tiny rock islands where sea lions lived. From there the canoes spread apart, each to a different island, and fishing was carried on separately with fishermen of just one village at each island.

Other celebrations, which included rituals and dances, were the Ten-Night Dance and the Flower Dance. Wealthy men paid for these events because it gave them the chance to wear their fancy clothes and expensive ornaments, and to treat the village and its guests to good food.

Village shamans played an important part in ritual events by dancing or being master of ceremonies. Shamans were mainly women in the Tolowa tribe. They were thought to be able to talk to the supernatural spirit-gods Tolowans believed lived all around them. More than being just spiritual doctors, however, the shamans' main jobs were as curing doctors for villagers.

Curing doctors believed all sickness came from a pain object that had entered the patient's body. They had many ways to take this 'pain' from an ill person, so that healing could begin. Actually, shamans were more like magicians of today, using sleight-of-hand tricks to pretend to remove objects that symbolized such a 'pain.'

Sometimes curing doctors would pretend to suck the pain out of a sick villager's body. They would bring an object, like a small stone or a stick, from their mouths, claiming it was the 'pain.' Fees for curing a person were always paid before the curing ritual even began. If someone died after a ritual, the shaman returned money or valuables paid to her earlier. Shamans charged very high fees to cure people.

Tribal myths were told to children by women storytellers. They were about the same supernatural animals that most tribes used in myths. There were tales of Coyote, Dog, Seagull, and Founder, who created the earth with its animals and people.

Redwood canoe,
see page 35.

FOOD

All four regions in Tolowa territory had some kind of food for tribal members. The ocean gave them many kinds of fish, shellfish, sea birds, and sea mammals like whales and sea lions. Plants along the grassy part of the shore furnished them with wild berries and tasty seaweed.

Although the redwood forest area had few plant foods, there were some deer and elk living there which furnished the tribal members with meat. Three different kinds of oak trees in the high valley region gave the tribe precious acorns for their main food.

The lower Smith River area had a great deal of food for Tolowa people. It was here that ducks, fish, and small animals lived. One of the best places in California for catching salmon was in this area. There were marshes where tule grew. Tule cane filled many needs the villagers had, from woven mats to clothing to tule sprouts, which were good to eat.

Acorns were gathered by women each autumn and stored in granaries in the permanent villages. Acorns were ground each day, as needed, and flour from them was made into either mush or bread. Stone mortars and pestles were used by the women to smash and grind acorn nutmeats. Chapter One, page 12, of this book tells how leaching of the acorn took out its bitter taste.

Many plant leaves and wild fruits were eaten fresh during the spring and summer. Those not eaten were usually dried for winter meals. Roots and bulbs were dug out of the ground with sharp-pointed three-foot-long sticks of hard mountain mahogany wood.

Sometimes the roots were cooked with water in boiling baskets using hot stones. The stones were tossed about the basket with a branch bent into a loop to keep the basket from getting burned.

Liddell 92

BASKETS AND TOOLS

Not only were baskets used for cooking, they were used in every part of Native American life. Large open-weave baskets were used for storage and to carry heavy loads on women's backs. More tightly woven baskets were used as eating bowls or to carry water.

Women wore basket hats on their heads, especially when carrying heavy burden baskets on their backs. A wide strap of woven fabric or buckskin was attached to both sides of a burden basket. This strap, or tumpline, went across the forehead of a woman to take some of the weight off her back. Basket hats kept the tumpline from pressing too hard on her forehead.

All Tolowa baskets were made by using the twined method of weaving. Baby cradles, trays and sifters, hoppers (bottomless baskets) glued onto mortars to keep bits of food from falling off as it was being ground, and small, pretty treasure baskets were all made by the tribal women.

Tools made by tribal men and boys were usually produced

in a certain area of the village. Here stone was shaped into adzes (curved axes), pounders, net sinkers (weights), and obsidian was flaked into sharp arrow points and knife blades. Cleaning fish and sea lions for meals was also done in this area.

Flint knife with attached wooden handle.

Wood was carved into knife handles, fine hunting bows, arrow shafts, and net floaters. Bone made excellent needles for sewing together tule mats, hooks for fishing, and whistles for accompanying dances. Many ornaments were made from bone. Animal antlers made fine wedges for splitting logs into planks.

Tolowa men made seagoing plank canoes that were built like the Yuroks' boats. Each canoe was carved from redwood with a raised bow (front) and stern (back). (See page 33.) Boats were also used in rivers and steered with paddles.

These well-built Tolowa boats were used in the ocean when deep-sea fishing and when hunting for sea lions. Sometimes the Tolowa fishermen took these canoes as far as eight miles into the ocean in their search for food.

CLOTHING

Women of this tribe wore a two-piece skirt as everyday clothing. The back piece, or apron, of the skirt was made of buckskin, large enough to wrap around the waist and almost meet in the front. The front apron was a narrow panel of plain buckskin. For celebrations and dancing, the women wore an apron front decorated with fringes and beads. (See page 37 for a picture.)

Men wore loincloths of buckskin or, like the children, went naked. On cooler days, and during the winter, men and women wore animal skin capes to keep warm.

Girls had their chins tattooed with three straight lines just before they became teenagers. This tattooed symbol showed to what family they belonged.

HISTORY

Tolowa tribal members first met white people in 1828 when they were visited by Jedediah Smith. The trader wrote of Tolowans as being great traders, dividing up products for trade into small packages and asking more for each package than all of them together were worth.

White traders brought new items, like metal knives, to Tolowans, but they also brought something else not needed by the tribe: disease. White peoples' diseases were deadly to Native Americans. They had no immunity to diseases like measles and cholera which killed tribal members by the thousands.

When settlers arrived to claim Tolowa territory, the tribespeople were so weak from illness, they had no strength to fight back. White soldiers stood up for American settlers against tribal members, killing many of them.

Some gold miners tore through the territory in the mid-1800s looking for gold, but found none. From 1908 to 1963, a reservation for tribal members who had lost their land and homes was kept near the mouth of the Klamath River.

Historians determine there were well over 1,000 Tolowa people before white people came. In 1960, a count showed under 300 still alive in Del Norte County, which used to be Tolowa land. Some of these 300 were not even Tolowans. In 1963 only ten full-blooded Tolowans could be found living there who could remember any useful history of old tribal living.

Today young, educated tribal members work in businesses in Crescent City. Many are working in large local lumber companies there. Some Tolowans have gone to San Francisco to live, where they can find jobs. There are little, if any, tribal events or customs followed these days.

A wealthy Tolowa woman wearing her finery including a beautiful string bead necklace.

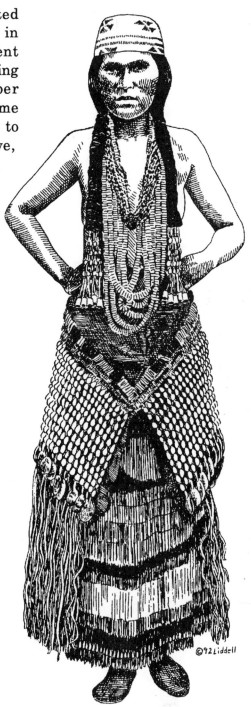

TOLOWA TRIBE
OUTLINE

I. Introduction
    A. Meaning of name
    B. Territory and boundaries
        1. Describe four regions
    C. Visiting between villages
    D. Permanent coastal homes

II. Villages
    A. Description of permanent dwelling houses
    B. Sweathouse descriptions
    C. Activity and work area

III. Village life
    A. Headman, how chosen
        1. Duties
    B. Importance of wealth to villagers
        1. Value of objects
        2. The value of daughters and bride price
    C. Crime and fines
        1. Adoption or 'slavery'
    D. Childbirth and child naming
    E. Teenage girls' ceremony
    F. Death rituals and customs
        1. Removal from death house
        2. Preparation of body

IV. Rituals and ceremonies
    A. Food rituals
        1. First sea-lion ceremony
    B. Other ritual and dance ceremonies

C. Shamans
    1. Master of ceremonies
    2. Curing doctors
        a. Pain objects
        b. Payments
D. Myths
V. Food
    A. Foods of four different regions
        1. Acorns and fresh plants
        2. Fish and animals
VI. Baskets and tools
    A. Baskets
        1. Uses and kinds of baskets
    B. Tools
        1. Stone
        2. Wood
        3. Bone
    C. Canoes
VII. Clothing
    A. Women's clothing
    B. Men's clothing
    C. Tattoos
VIII. History
    A. First meeting of white people
    B. White people's diseases
    C. White settlers
    D. Goldminers
    E. Reservations
    F. Population of tribe then and now
    G. Tolowans today

GLOSSARY

AWL: a sharp, pointed tool used for making small holes in leather or wood

CEREMONY: a meeting of people to perform formal rituals for a special reason; like an awards ceremony to hand out trophies to those who earned honors

CHERT: rock which can be chipped off, or flaked, into pieces with sharp edges

COILED: a way of weaving baskets which looks like the basket is made of rope coils woven together

DIAMETER: the length of a straight line through the center of a circle

DOWN: soft, fluffy feathers

DROUGHT: a long period of time without water

DWELLING: a building where people live

FLETCHING: attaching feathers to the back end of an arrow to make the arrow travel in a straight line

GILL NET: a flat net hanging vertically in water to catch fish by their heads and gills

GRANARIES: basket-type storehouses for grains and nuts

HERITAGE: something passed down to people from their long-ago relatives

LEACHING: washing away a bitter taste by pouring water through foods like acorn meal

MORTAR: flat surface of wood or stone used for the grinding of grains or herbs with a pestle

PARCHING:	to toast or shrivel with dry heat
PESTLE:	a small stone club used to mash, pound, or grind in a mortar
PINOLE:	flour made from ground corn
INDIAN RESERVATION:	land set aside for Native Americans by the United States government
RITUAL:	a ceremony that is always performed the same way
SEINE NET:	a net which hangs vertically in the water, encircling and trapping fish when it is pulled together
SHAMAN:	tribal religious men or women who use magic to cure illness and speak to spirit-gods
SINEW:	stretchy animal tendons
STEATITE:	a soft stone (soapstone) mined on Catalina Island by the Gabrielino tribe; used for cooking pots and bowls
TABOO:	something a person is forbidden to do
TERRITORY:	land owned by someone or by a group of people
TRADITION:	the handing down of customs, rituals, and belief, by word of mouth or example, from generation to generation
TREE PITCH:	a sticky substance found on evergreen tree bark
TWINING:	a method of weaving baskets by twisting fibers, rather than coiling them around a support fiber

NATIVE AMERICAN WORDS
WE KNOW AND USE

PLANTS AND TREES
hickory
pecan
yucca
mesquite
saguaro

ANIMALS
caribou
chipmunk
cougar
jaguar
opossum
moose

STATES
Dakota – friend
Ohio – good river
Minnesota – waters that
  reflect the sky
Oregon – beautiful water
Nebraska – flat water
Arizona
Texas

FOODS
avocado
hominy
maize (corn)
persimmon
tapioca
succotash

GEOGRAPHY
bayou – marshy body of
  water
savannah – grassy plain
pasadena – valley

WEATHER
blizzard
Chinook (warm, dry wind)

FURNITURE
hammock

HOUSE
wigwam
wickiup
tepee
igloo

INVENTIONS
toboggan

BOATS
canoe
kayak

OTHER WORDS
caucus – group meeting
mugwump – loner politician
squaw – woman
papoose – baby

CLOTHING
moccasin
parka
mukluk – slipper
poncho

BIBLIOGRAPHY

Cressman, L. S. *Prehistory of the Far West.* Salt Lake City, Utah: University of Utah Press, 1977.

Geiger, Maynard, O.F.M., Ph.D. *The Indians of Mission Santa Barbara.* Santa Barbara, CA 93105: Franciscan Fathers, 1986.

Heizer, Robert F., volume editor. *Handbook of North American Indians; California, volume 8.* Washington, D.C.: Smithsonian Institute, 1978.

Heizer, Robert F. and Elsasser, Albert B. *The Natural World of the California Indians.* Berkeley and Los Angeles, CA; London, England: University of California Press, 1980.

Heizer, Robert F. and Whipple, M.A.. *The California Indians.* Berkeley and Los Angeles, CA; London, England: University of California Press, 1971.

Heuser, Iva. *California Indians.* PO Box 352, Camino, CA 95709: Sierra Media Systems, 1977.

Macfarlen, Allen and Paulette. *Handbook of American Indian Games.* 31 E. 2nd Street, Mineola, N.Y. 11501: Dover Publications, 1985.

Murphey, Edith Van Allen. *Indian Uses of Native Plants.* 603 W. Perkins Street, Ukiah, CA 95482: Mendocino County Historical Society, © renewal, 1987.

National Geographic Society. *The World of American Indians.* Washington, DC: National Geographic Society reprint, 1989.

Tunis, Edwin. *Indians.* 2231 West 110th Street, Cleveland, OH: The World Publishing Company, 1959.

Credits:
Island Industries, Vashon Island, Washington 98070
Dona McAdam, Mac on the Hill, Seattle, Washington 98109

Acknowledgements:
Kim Walters, Library Director, and Richard Buchen,
Research Librarian, Braun Library, Southwest Museum
Special thanks

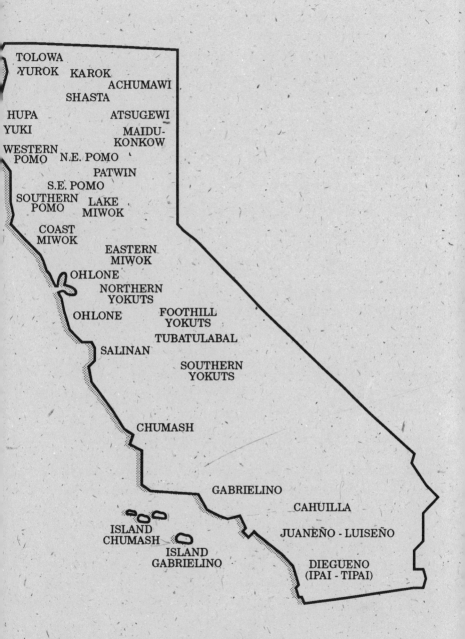

TOLOWA
YUROK KAROK
ACHUMAWI
SHASTA
HUPA ATSUGEWI
YUKI MAIDU-
KONKOW
WESTERN
POMO N.E. POMO
PATWIN
S.E. POMO
SOUTHERN LAKE
POMO MIWOK
COAST
MIWOK
EASTERN
MIWOK
OHLONE
NORTHERN
YOKUTS
OHLONE FOOTHILL
YOKUTS
TUBATULABAL
SALINAN
SOUTHERN
YOKUTS

CHUMASH

GABRIELINO
CAHUILLA
JUANEÑO - LUISEÑO
ISLAND
CHUMASH
ISLAND
GABRIELINO
DIEGUENO
(IPAI - TIPAI)

Map Art: Dona McAdam

At last, a detailed book on the
Tolowa Tribe
written just for students

Mary Null Boulé taught in the California
public school system for twenty-five years.
Her teaching years made her aware of the
acute need for well-researched regional
social studies books for elementary school
students. This series on the California
Native American tribes fills a long-standing
need in California education. Ms. Boulé is
also author and publisher of *The Missions:
California's Heritage*. She is married and
the mother of five grown children.

Illustrator Daniel Liddell has been creating
artistic replicas of Native American arti-
facts for several years, and his paintings
reflect his own Native American heritage.
His paternal grandmother was full-blood
Chickasaw.

ISBN: 1-877599-43-3